Juan and Gwen's
BIG FUNDRAISING SURPRISE

By STAN LEVENSON

Illustrations by Ifat Naim

9/17/17

Dear Hannah, Noah,
Elijah & Isaiah,
Please enjoy my
new book.
Have a wonderful
school year.
With love,
Stan Levenson

To Kay
One of the Best Reading Teachers of All Time

Juan and Gwen's school had broken fences, broken computers and leaking water faucets. The heaters didn't heat and the air conditioners didn't cool. When Juan and Gwen were thirsty, the drinking fountains dribbled warm water.

The books and materials were so tattered and torn that the kids had a hard time figuring out the beginning and end of a story. In addition, when it rained the holes in the playground would fill up with so much water that the ducks from a nearby park would come over for a swim.

Everywhere Juan and Gwen looked, the school needed fixing.

"What can we do to help our school?" asked Juan.

Gwen replied, "I've been thinking about it for a long time. Let's ask our teacher, Mrs. Marcus, if we could have a yard sale at the school. Our neighbors had a yard sale last month and made enough money to go on a vacation to Mexico. If we have a yard sale we could use the money we earn to fix up our school."

"That sounds like a great idea," replied Juan.

Juan and Gwen ran off to see Mrs. Marcus. They were very excited about their idea.

"Mrs. Marcus, we want to have a yard sale to help our school become a better place for learning," said Gwen.

"What do you mean?" responded Mrs. Marcus.

"The books and materials are old, the heaters won't heat, the air conditioners won't cool, the computers don't work and we can't play on the playground after it rains," said Juan.

"I love your idea, " responded Mrs. Marcus, but first we have to get permission from Dr. Perez, our Principal."

All three, Juan, Gwen, and Mrs. Marcus, went off to see the Principal.

"Dr. Perez, Juan and Gwen want to have a yard sale at the school. They would like to use the money they earn to fix things up including the water fountains, the heaters, the air conditioners, and the holes in the playground. They also want to help replace some of the tattered books and materials as well as the computers, and software," explained Mrs. Marcus.

"Do you know it's going to cost a lot of money to do all these things?" explained Dr. Perez.
"We knew it would," said Juan.
"We also know that it is going to be a lot of hard work too," said Gwen.

"Well, I'll tell you what we can do. You can use the school in two weeks on Saturday for your yard sale, and I'll be one of your first customers," said Dr. Perez.

"Wow," shouted Gwen.

"Great," yelled Juan.

Juan and Gwen both knew that the task ahead of them was going to be very difficult but very important. They also knew that they didn't have much time to get ready.

The first person Juan and Gwen went to see for help and suggestions was Granny Garcia. The kids called her Granny because she was a lot older than everyone else.

Granny volunteered at the school library each day and was one of the nicest people around. She loved to bake cookies for the kids and read them wonderful stories. In addition, Granny was also a graduate of the school many years ago when it first opened. She is what some people call an alumna of the school or part of the alumni.

"Granny, Gwen and I need your help and expertise," said Juan. "We are having a yard sale at the school in two weeks on Saturday and want to sell things and raise enough money to make the school look like new again.."

"Kids, that's a wonderful idea." Granny Garcia replied.

"Do you have any suggestions on how to do it?" asked Juan.

"Yes I do," said Granny. "First, you have to convince a lot of parents that there is a need for the sale. Then you have to get lots of people involved in looking for items to sell. Next, you have to get permission from the kid's parents to allow them to be involved in the yard sale. Then, you have to let the people know about the sale and arrange to pick up the items that will be sold. And finally, you have to decide how much you are going to sell each item for," explained Granny Garcia.

"Wow, that's a lot of work but we can do it," said Gwen.

"Absolutely," responded Juan.

"By the way, I want to be the first volunteer to work with you on this. Did you know that I graduated from this school many years ago?" said Granny.

"I didn't know that," said Gwen.

"Did the school look so bad when you went here?" asked Juan.

"No, in fact the school just opened when I went here. It was shiny new," said Granny. "I definitely want to help you so that we can make this school look brand new again."

"Hooray, we always knew you would help us," said Juan.

The next day during nutrition and lunch break, Juan and Gwen asked a lot of kids at the school if they wanted to help with the yard sale in two weeks on Saturday. The response was overwhelming. Most agreed to help.

Dr. Perez also announced the yard sale on the school's public address system, which fortunately happened to be working that day.

Permission slips were prepared and sent home with the children.

Much to everyone's surprise, more than 350 kids brought their signed permission slips back to school the next day.

"I can't believe this," Juan said.

"I knew we would get a good response," Gwen replied.

On Thursday after school, the kids who volunteered and brought back signed permission slips were told by Juan and Gwen to report to Granny Garcia in the library in two shifts after school. It was very crowded at each shift but everyone was happy and eager to learn what they were going to do next.

Granny divided everyone into teams of two and gave them instructions on what to say and do when they went to people's homes to ask for donated items.

"Make sure to be polite when you meet people and don't forget to say 'thank you' for all donated items." said Granny.

"Also invite your parents to accompany you. It's a lot safer that way."

The kids were very happy with Granny's instructions and were eager to participate.

Parents with trucks and cars volunteered to pick up and bring the big items to school with their kids on Thursday before the sale. You wouldn't believe what they came back with? Some came with books. Others brought bicycles, games, skates, toys and clothing. Another group arrived with paintings, fishing poles, tennis racquets, bats, baseballs, basketballs, and gloves. A third group came with computers, printers, cell phones, software, and T.V.s.

As the day turned into evening, it started to rain real hard. It continued to rain on Friday, the day before the big event. Juan and Gwen had to make certain to keep all items out of the rain. They began to worry that they might have to cancel the sale if it rained on Saturday.

"Don't worry," said Granny Garcia. "I believe it's going to be a very sunny day tomorrow."

When Saturday morning arrived, not only was it a sunny day, but more than 500 people showed up for the sale, and what a sale it was. People were buying things like crazy. Eventually, every single item sold.

To everyone's surprise, especially Juan and Gwen's, a group of kids brought their piggy banks and spare coins to donate to the school. Another group of parents, teachers, retired teachers, and a retired principal wrote checks to the school or contributed cash. Granny Garcia wrote a check as well.

"Wow," this is unbelievable," Juan cried out.

"I never expected all of this. What a surprise," shouted Gwen.

"This was a great team effort headed up by Juan and Gwen," said Granny with a smile on her face and tears in her eyes.

Juan and Gwen were overwhelmed with joy.

"What a day this has been," exclaimed Juan.

"All this hard work has really paid off," Gwen shouted.

Granny Garcia, Mrs. Marcus, and Dr. Perez were overwhelmed with joy.

As the big day was coming to an end, Juan and Gwen helped Granny Garcia, Mrs. Marcus and Dr. Perez count the money they made from the donated items. They also counted the cash, the monies from the piggy banks, coin collections, and the checks that were written. It was unbelievable. They raised more than $50,000.

"What an achievement," said Granny Garcia.

"This is wonderful," shouted Mrs. Marcus.

Dr. Perez fell out of his chair in disbelief.

Juan, trying not to laugh as Dr. Perez was getting up from the floor asked, "Dr. Perez, how many things can we fix at the school with the money we raised?"

"I believe we can fix just about everything," said Dr. Perez. "Our School Board is going to be very happy. I will make certain that everything gets fixed."

Everyone grabbed Juan and Gwen and hugged them until they almost couldn't breathe.

Dr. Perez said, "Juan and Gwen, we are so delighted with what you have accomplished. I am going to have an outdoor assembly on Monday morning and announce the good news to all the parents, the faculty, the kids, and the total school community."

"Oh, that would be wonderful," said Gwen.

On Monday morning at the outdoor assembly Dr. Perez welcomed everyone. He started by saying, "We have some very good news for all of you. On Saturday, with your help and the help of our entire student body we raised more than $50,000."

The audience gasped in disbelief. They never thought they could raise so much money. Everyone applauded with gusto.

"This is a wonderful accomplishment," said Dr. Perez. "I want to particularly thank two of our students who were instrumental in making Saturday such a huge success. Will Juan Gonzalez and Gwen Smith come forward? Let's give them a big round of applause."

Everyone started to applaud loudly including Granny Garcia, Mrs. Marcus, the parents, the faculty, the students, and the entire school community.

The ovation was heard six blocks away.

Juan and Gwen were a little embarrassed by all the attention they were getting.

"Do you want to say something Juan and Gwen?" said Dr. Perez.

Juan stepped forward and said, "I can't believe how we raised so much money on Saturday. There were so many people who contributed so many items to sell. In addition, lots of kids brought in their piggy banks and coin collections to contribute. Also, many parents, teachers, and graduates of this school contributed cash and wrote checks. This is great school spirit."

"It also shows a lot of love for our school," said Gwen.

After the assembly was over, the parents headed home and the kids went back to their classrooms.

Dr. Perez said to Juan, Gwen, Granny Garcia and Mrs. Marcus "Can we all meet tomorrow morning in the library about 7:30 A.M. before school starts?"

"I would be very happy to," said Mrs. Marcus.

"I'll be there," said Granny Garcia.

Juan and Gwen agreed to meet as well.

The next morning bright and early, Juan, Gwen, Mrs. Marcus, Dr. Perez and Granny Garcia met.

Dr. Perez started the meeting by welcoming everyone and then said, "I'm so happy with the money raised on Saturday that I talked to the Superintendent about starting the work early next week and would like all of you there when we start."

"I would be excited to come," said Gwen.

"That's for sure," responded Juan.

Granny Garcia raised her hand and said, "Last night I thought a lot about the school and when I went here as a student. I remember all of the great teachers that I had and how they influenced my life. I love this place with all my heart and that's why I also wrote a check. I think we should plan on something special for Juan and Gwen who were so vital in raising all the funds."

"We don't need anything special," said Juan.

"Just accomplishing the big fundraising effort was very special for us," said Gwen.

Granny continued and said, "Juan and Gwen have done so much for this school. Being a graduate, I would like to recommend that a permanent plaque be displayed in the main hallway of the school. I'm suggesting that the plaque read something like this."

THIS PLAQUE IS A TRIBUTE TO
JUAN GONZALES & GWEN SMITH
WHO WERE MOST INFLUENTIAL
IN RAISING MORE THAN
$50,000
FOR THE SCHOOL.

CONGRATULATIONS!

"I'm in complete agreement with your idea," said Dr. Perez.
"Unbelievable!" cried Juan.
"This makes me so happy," Gwen shouted.

Mrs. Marcus said, "I am so proud you are my students. You have done so much for this school."

Dr. Perez was smiling from ear to ear.

Everyone jumped up and hugged Juan and Gwen again and again.

Dr. Perez said, "You started all of this. You are two special kids."

They all held hands. Everyone had tears in their eyes, and Juan, Gwen, Granny, Mrs. Marcus, and Dr. Perez had smiles on their faces dreaming how the school was going to look when it got all fixed up.

This was Juan and Gwen's big fundraising surprise.

At the conclusion of all the excitement Gwen said, "This experience taught me a lot about fundraising and emphasized how important everyone is in working together as a team to raise needed monies for our school. I loved every minute of it."

Juan shook his head in agreement and said, "I will always remember the generosity of our school community. It will live within me forever."

52246433R00023

Made in the USA
San Bernardino, CA
15 August 2017